A Collection of 50 Spells

For Simple & Powerful Magick

Witchcraft Magick

#1 Protection Chant

Here is a protection chant to protect you from evil, you should do this before and after doing spells.

Visualize yourself sitting in the middle of the pentagram facing upwards with 3 circles of purple light round you and say:

*"PROTECT ME WITH ALL YOUR MIGHT,
OH GODDESS ,
GRACIOUS DAY AND NIGHT"*

Say it three times then end it with

"SO MOTE IT BE"

Another version of the same spell just different words is:

*"THRICE AROUND THE CIRCLE'S BOUND
SINK ALL EVIL TO THE GROUND"*

Say it three times and end it with

"SO MOTE IT BE"

#2 Protection Spell

Protection chant for out-door spells:
Before attempting spells at night, out-doors, take up a
blessed object (wand for instance) and draw a
pentagrams in the air.
Imagine the pentagram glowing and the evil around
being trapped inside until after your spells, chant:

Hail fair moon
Ruler of the night;
Guard me and mine
Until the light

#3 To Break A Curse

Take five white candles and arrange them in a
pentagram.
Place a black candle, which symbolizes the curse, in its
center.
The ones afflicted by the curse must speak the words
revealed here:

Evil curse that blights out lives
Be lifted now and flee
These candles' lights overcome the dark
From its grasps, set us free

#4 A Purification Spell

To be used when feeling depressed, out of control of your life, after the breaking of a relationship and at any other time when you feel the need.

Take four coins.
Wash them just until they're sparkling clean (you may need to scrub them with baking soda and a toothbrush).
Do this before going to the well.
Stand before the well facing West.

Toss a coin into the well, saying:

I freely give this up.

Move so that you're facing North before the well.

Toss a coin into it, saying:

I freely give this up.

Now facing East before the well, toss and say:

I freely give this up.

Facing South, throw a coin into the well and say:

I freely give this up.

Your rite has ended.

(Note: it would be unwise to perform this ritual in a well actually used as a source of drinking water.)

#5 For Beauty

Beauty isn't in the eye of the beholder, it's a reflection of our feelings about ourselves. When we dwell on our "defects" (no human body is perfect), we lessen our inward and outward beauty.

This ritual is designed to increase our good feelings for ourselves, which is reflected in the image we present to others. Thus, it increases beauty.

This is a simple rite.

Hold five pennies in your projective hand.
Visualize yourself as a beautiful person.

Don't see yourself as your favorite movie stars, who have make-up artists, lighting directors and cinematographers to assisted them.

Visualize yourself as a loving, open person radiating beauty.

Pour this image into the pennies.

Toss one into the well while saying:

I allow myself to be beautiful.
I accept beauty.

Repeat this with the remaining four coins.

It is done.

#6 Attraction Spell

You take a red or pink candle scented oil(or perfume but oil is recommended) which is your favorite, and you taker a piece of red construction paper, or plain white paper and color it red, and cut out a heart.

You turn out all lights and make sure your away from anything that will cause disturbance.

You light the candle (turn off the lights) put it in the center of the paper heart, drip a couple of drops of the oil on the heart and say:

"May the corn stone of my affections
be grace and goodness,
and let my love know no boundary,
for the greater my love for others,
so in kind will that love come back to me."

And that should attract love, if you want love from a certain someone, you should say:

"I Love _(Name of person)_"

ten times after repeating the last verse.

God bless thee all.

#7 For Driving Away Evil

Demons and evil spirits could be forced to leave a person alone if the following spell was written on parchment or paper which was to be kept close at hand at all times.

SDPNQCN
DPNQCN
PNQCN
NQCN
QCN
CN
N

#8 For A Safe Return

**In a small bag of supple leather or brown cloth,
assemble these:**
a stone the size of a pigeon's egg,
a spoonful of ash from the morning hearth,
a chip of bark from the tallest tree,
a pinch of earth,
a curl of dust,
a blade of grass,
(all gathered from the place you leave)
Add a lodestone or small magnet,
tie the bag with a strip of vine;
wear it around your neck, on a thong --
then do not grieve,
you must return.

#9 For Success

Steep in a bath a bowlful of leaves from three or four or five of these:

Marigold,
Celery,
Mint and Grass,
Nasturtium,
Parsley,
Fennel and Cress.
(Calendula, Telina, Menta si Iarba,)

When the Brew is green, and the steam is sweet, lie in the water and thrice repeat:

I shall bathe and I shall be
as green and strong, good Herbs, as thee.
Draw me favor, draw me fame,
Draw bright honor to my name

Rise from the water thrice empowered;
Wear those virtues you have conjured.

#10 Spell To Remember A Past Life:

Items needed:
1 white candle,
1 mirror;

Sit in front of the mirror, turn off the lights and light the candle.

Set the candle next to the mirror so the light from it can hit your face, but so you will not see the candle in the mirror.

After this is done, look into your eyes and say:

"Oracle of lunar light,
Send me the second sight."

Stare into your eyes and do not blink.

Your reflection will dissolve and another will appear.

Try to look at the face, body, clothing and surroundings.

After you do this you will have emotions you cannot explain.

Don't worry... they go away in a few minutes.

#11 Full Moon Wishing Spell:

At night, when the moon is full, go outside with a glass of juice.

Look up at the moon and tell her exactly what you desire (do this in full detail and don't leave anything out!).

When you are done, lift your glass in toast to the moon and say:

"Mother Goddess, look and see
This goblet that I offer Thee
It is Yours for all You do
Gracious One of silver hue"

Pour the juice on the ground and know that your wish will be granted.

#12 To Be Revenged On One Who Has Done You Harm

This spell is to be used with caution, because, it is rather important to decide at which point in time you will want it to take hold.

This is particularly good for when you are viewed as the "Loser" and your opponent is viewed as the "Winner":

**Spell to exchange the Luck with a
Person who has vexed you....**

1. Determine a particular possession that the person is particularly fond of; his automobile, his garden, his boat, his favorite chair, etc.

2. Then on the day of a full moon (i.e. full moon at night or full moon in the day), cut a length of blackberry (bramble) vine.

It is EXTREMELY important that YOU do not touch the piece of vine, lest the spell backfire.

Carry it with a garden or some other kind of tool.

3. By sunset lay it carefully under the person's beloved object and chant:

Cerridwin's vine, Cerridwin's vine!
Thine will be that of mine!
By the power of three times three!
By the power I conjure in me!

Our lucks shall change hands!
Mine is his and his mine!
By the power so Devine!
So mote it be in spoken bands!

Gradually your luck will change.
Should the victim pick up the vine or touch it, he will
have bad luck, and you will have good luck.

If he injures himself on the thorns, he will suffer an
accident, and you will come to money.

But this of course, depends on how much good or bad
luck your "victim" has.

He will suffer your fate, you shall suffer his.

Like all spells, this one must be used with prudence,
since you are not cursing, you are exchanging
something using magick.

The luck exchange holds a year and a day, and cannot be
counteracted.

#13 A Spell Of Protection

Sit or stand before any fire.

Look into the flames (or flame, if using a candle).

Visualize the fire bathing you with glowing, protective light.

The fire creates a flaming, shimmering sphere around you.

If you wish, say the following or similar words:

"Craft the spell in the fire;
Craft it well;
Weave it higher.
Weave it now of shining flame;
None shall come to hurt or maim.
None shall pass this fiery wall;
None shall pass No,
none at all."

Repeat this simple yet effective ritual every day when in need.

#14 Purification Ritual

Materials needed:
White candle
Fire-proof vessel
Paper
Writing utensil
Purifying oils
Blanket

Begin the ritual by taking a hot bath with purifying oils added to the water.

Oils to try would be lemon and eucalyptus.

Have the white candle lit in the bathroom with you.

Visualize the negativity leaving your body and mingling in the water.

Visualize this negativity being cleansed and returning to you in a positive form.

Once you feel calm and at peace, dress in a special robe or article of clothing.

If you choose to remain sky clad that is also fine.

With the candle walk to your front door.

You will be purifying each entrance to your home moving clockwise throughout the house or apartment.

While walking chant:

Darkness flee from this light
Be gone from my sight

Once all entrances have been purified, find a comfortable place in your home to finish the rest of the ritual.

In this place you should have enough room for you to lay down comfortably.

It is also necessary to be within sight of the white candle, so pick an area where fire hazards would be at a minimum.

You will first need to cleanse yourself of any negative emotions that may have built up over the years.

Write down these feelings on the paper.

Be honest and specific.

Do not stop until you feel you have expressed it all.

Once you are done writing use the candle to light the paper on fire.

Place this in a fire proof vessel and watch it burn.

Visualize the cleansing of the fire and a new and happier you rising from the flames.

Chant:
Fire burns away old

Wrap yourself in the blanket, as if in a cocoon.

Be sure to leave an opening for your mouth and nose.
Lie down and feel yourself relax.

Feel yourself sink into the earth.

Tonight marks the beginning of a new way of life.

For a beginning to occur, death must also.

Feel yourself return to the earth, become part of it,
nourish it.

Pour out the last of your pain and suffering.

Let the Lady and the Lord comfort you in this dark
place.

Do not force things to occur.

Simply allow emotions to take control.

You must purge the pain and suffering and allow the
happiness to guide you.
Listen to all that you hear.

Take note, for there are important lessons to be learned.

Once you feel yourself free of the pain and being guided by peace and happiness, begin to wiggle out of the blanket.

Do not unfold or unwrap it, but will out of it as if it was the birth canal.

Remember you are being reborn.

Once out, survive all around you.

See the positive, see the peace.

Be sure to thank every presence that helped you be reborn.

#15 Money Spell

(Said while making
9 knots in green,
13-inch silk cord or ribbon)

By knot of one, my spell's begun
By knot of two, plenty fruitful work to do
By knot of three, money comes to me
By knot of four, opportunity knocks at my door
By knot of five, my business thrives
By knot of six, this spell is fixed
By knot of seven, success is given
By knot of eight, increase is great
By knot of nine, these things are mine

Prosperity Oil

This classic prosperity oil has been used for at least 100 years.

It is best made on a Thursday and is believed to be most effective if allowed to sit for three weeks after mixing.

A small green piece of fabric may be anointed with the oil and carried in the purse.

The oil may be worn as a perfume.

Omit the base oil if you wish to use with aromatherapy oil warmer. Sunflower, or light mineral.

Mix all ingredients carefully and put into a dark glass
bottle.

Allow it to sit for at least three weeks then strain
through cheesecloth or muslin to remove the basil
powder residue.

Keep a small coin in the bottle and keep away from
direct sunlight.

#16 The Bottle Spell

(variation of the traditional witch's bottle)

This spell can be used to neutralize the power of those who intend to hurt your reputation, in any way pose a threat to your security, or who want to do you physical harm.

Tools:
black thread
black ink or black ballpoint pin
parchment paper
1 bottle with a cork or mortar and pestle
1 white candle
4 tablespoons orris-root (or oak moss)
4 tablespoons sea salt
4 tablespoons black powdered iron (available at pottery shops where ironstone is made)
4 tablespoons frankincense or myrrh

Mix the sea salt, orris-root powder, and iron in a bowl.

Then cut a piece of parchment to fit inside your bottle and write on it in black ink:

*I neutralize the power of [name of your adversary]
to do me any harm.
I ask that this be correct and for the good of all.
So mote it be.*

Roll up the parchment, tie it with black thread to bind it, and place it in the bottle.

Fill the bottle with the dry ingredients.

Then take the white candle and, while turning the bottle counterclockwise, drip the wax over the top to seal it.

Last, secretly bury the bottle in a place where it will not be disturbed and no animal or person will dig it up.

It should never be opened or the power of the spell is lost.

#17 Prosperity Spell

You need:
some money or pictures of cash, checks and jewels
(to be placed on the altar)
drums for raising energy

Put the money on the altar, not as an object to worship but as a symbol to your deep mind of what you want to obtain.

You may wish to place a goddess statue or another religious symbol behind the symbolic wealth, as a reminder that money is not after the ultimate value.

Then, stand up, and drum and chant to raise power.

Your chant can be something like :

Wealth , wealth ,come to me ,
I deserve prosperity.

As the power moves toward its peak , imagine a huge transparent funnel over you, and huge amounts of cash, checks and other forms of wealth cascading down though it to pile up around you (or at least, enough for your needs + some to donate to worthy causes).

Give thanks for the wealth which you know will be headed your way.

Open the circle.

Afterwards, go seek a job if you don't have one or ask for a raise, and always give money to charities.

Soon prosperity will come to you.

#18 Nightmare Spells

I was plagued by the same bad dream night after night for over a month and I decided to do something about it.

This spell was given to me by a fellow witch's grandmother (who is also a witch) and I elaborated on it.

Items required:
scarf (white or cream colors work best)
4 cloves
pinch of basil
pinch of ground sage
lavender or vanilla oil (whatever you find more soothing)
black marker
white ribbon

Lay the scarf out.
You will be putting spices into it.

Place the spices (ground sage, 4 cloves, basil) into the scarf and add 2 drops of oil.

Gather the scarf at the top (like a moneybag) and tie it with the ribbon.

On the outside of the scarf draw the nightmare that plagues you (e.g. spiders, falling)

Place the scarf under your pillow and sleep with it there.

#19 Three Times Three Spell

To have someone see his errors:

This is a three times three spell to use on people who were corrupt in their ways.

It has no negative consequence unless you think ill of the person while casting the spell.

Wind in the north, run through the trees
Three times three, let them see, let them see
Sands of the east, rich soils beneath
Three times three, set them free, set them free
Fires in the south, awaken from sleep
Three times three, let them see, let them see
Water of the west, flow to the seas
Three times three, set them free, set them free

It works best if you have something representing that person, like a strand of their hair or a fingernail.

The spell may not work instantaneously, you may have to repeat it for the person to see error in their ways.

Please be sure you're not being hypocritical, because that may cause negative feedback..

So, all warnings given, blessed be!

#20 To Bind A Trouble Maker

BEST TIME: Waning Moon

Situate the cauldron between 2 black candles, with a third black candle opposite you on the far side of the altar.

Burn a protection or binding incense.

Have the names of your enemies written on a small peice of parchment.

If the names are unknown, merely write all my enemies.

Sprinkle basil and elder flowers into the cauldron.

Say:
Bubble, bubble, cauldron bubble
Burn the evil, destroy the trouble.

Ignite the parchment from the central candle and drop into the cauldron.

Take up the wand and stir the air above the cauldron while chanting:

Darkness ended, control is done.
Light has come. My battle's won.

Take the ashes and herbs outside.

Throw them up to the winds and the Moon

#21 To Gain Prophecies

BEST TIME: Waxing Moon

Fill the cauldron half-full of water and place it on a table where you can see comfortably into it while seated.

Light 2 purple candles and a good divination incense; a combination of mugwort and wormwood work well.

Arrange the candles so their light does not shine into the water in your eyes.

Focus your attention on the bottom of the cauldron, your hands placed lightly on either side.

Breathe gently into the water and say:

Cauldron,
reveal to me that which I seek
Great Mother,
open my inner eye that I may truly see.

Empty your mind as much as possible; remain relaxed while looking deep into the cauldron waters.

The answer may come in images in the water, picture in your mind and strong bursts of "knowing".

#22 Money Spell Bottle

Items needed:
5 old pennies
5 dimes
5 quarters (or, five each of three denominations of your
country's coin currency, if outside the United States)
5 kernels of dried corn
5 sesame seeds
5 cinnamon sticks
5 cloves
5 whole allspice
5 pecans

Place each item into a thin, tall bottle, such as a spice
bottle. Cap it tightly.

Shake the bottle with your projective hand for five
minutes while chanting these or similar words:

Herbs and silver,
Copper and grain;
Work to increase
My money gain.

Place the money spell bottle on a table somewhere in
your house.

Leave your purse, pocketbook, wallet and/or checkbook
near the bottle when at home.

Allow money to come into your life.
It is done.

#23 To Make Your Partner More Passionate In Bed

Write his or her name on a red phallus candle, stroke it 9 times with musk oil, and then pass it through the smoke of musk incense.

Light the candle once a day, letting it burn 1/2 an inch each time.

When the candle is finished, wrap it in a piece of red satin and keep it under your bed for one month.

#24 Vexation Box

This spell is for dealing with someone who is more of an annoyance than a threat.

Someone who really gets on your nerves or stresses you out by intruding in your life or violating your space.

It is for someone you have already asked to stop but who persists in bothering you.

It is not a spell to use on someone whose actions you object to within their own life or space.

You need:
a box
two heads of garlic (or more, if you are using a big box or dealing with a group of people)
herbs of protection
a photograph of the person, or their name written on a piece of paper

Put everything in the box.

Cover the box and give it a good hard shake, mentally yelling at the person to modify the behavior that annoys you.

Put the box away, in a drawer or up on a shelf.

Take it out and give it a hard shake, yelling at them, every time they annoy you.

After the first week or so you should seldom need to
shake the box.

Throw the box away in a few months, when the garlic
begins to spoil.

#25 To Protect An Object

With the first and middle fingers, trace a pentagram
over the object to be protected.

Visualize electric-blue or purple flame streaming from
your fingers to form the pentagram.

Say this as you trace:

*"With this pentagram I lay
Protection here both night and day.
And the one who should not touch let his fingers burn and
twitch.
I now invoke the law of three:
This is my will, so mote it be!"*

#26 Glamour Spell

You will need:
1 wine glass of water
1 pinch of salt
1 red candle
1 light blue candle
1 red rose (no scars or imperfections for best results)
1 round hand-held mirror

Procedure:
Drop the pinch of salt into the glass of water saying:
"Beauty be within me.
Beauty now set me free."

Carve the symbol of sex into the red candle.

Carve a mirror symbol into the light blue one.

Light the two candles, first the light blue one and then
the red.

Lay the mirror between the two candles and scry into
your reflection.

Drop the rose petals one by one onto the mirror.

After this is done, drink the water and say:
"Beauty, beauty come to me.
Beauty, beauty set me free.

Let the candles burn down all the way. "

#27 Spell to Restore Peace to an Unhappy Home

Tools:
Black candle.
Astral candles of those in the home: Yellow-green candle.
Light blue candle.
Deity candles – ex. white and black, or Gold and Silver.
Incense- frankincense is good.
Votive candle - white is good.

Method:
Light Deity Candles and the incense.
Sit and meditate on the goal to be accomplished.
Light the Astral Candles of those in the home, which are placed approximately 13" from each other.
Think hard of each person, saying as the Candles are lit:

*"This candle represents <Name> .
As it burns, so burns his/her spirit."*

Write down the faults and problems that beset the home.

Discuss them with the others.
Then light the Votive Candle, visualizing the start of a new day and new turn for the better, e.g. visualize turning over an old brown leaf and finding it green and vibrant on the other side.
Light the Yellow-Green Candle (for Anger, and Jealousy and Discord).

Say:

"Here burns away all negative emotions from
<Name> and <Name>, leaving only love and happiness.
It is in our house; it is all about us.
There is tranquility in our home.
Peace and love abound and are with us.
For true happiness now is known.
Understanding and love are there in abundance; discord
and chaos are fled.
For be it ever thus, that as patience and love do grow and
prosper,
So barren become the fields of doubt and distress.
Happiness is the light that burns and darkness all away is
sent.
The home is peace; peace is the home."

Meditate for 3-5 minutes on settling the disturbed conditions in the home.

Now hold up the paper containing the problems, and burn it in the Votive Candle.

Visualize all the problems vanishing.

Move the Astral Candles closer to each other.

Light the Black Candle (for Destruction of Negativity).

Repeat the words, then meditate for 3-5 minutes on the problems having gone.

Move the Astral Candles further closer to each other.

Light the Light Blue Candle (for Peace and Understanding).

Finally repeat the words once more, then meditate for another 3-5 minutes on the new peaceful condition of the home.

Move the Astral candles even closer to each other.

Hug and kiss each other and call out "Hurrah" or other such words expressing joy and relief and victory.

Then extinguish the Votive Candle, and then the Astral and Day candles.

Note: The spell is even more powerful if it is repeated on 3 consecutive days, with different day candles, and letting the Astral candles touch each other only at the third incantation on the third day.

There is no need to write down the problems on the second or third day.

However, the spell may be only performed once, in which case, the Astral candles should touch other at the third incantation.

The ashes of the "problem paper" can be gleefully flushed down the toilet.

#28 Good Luck Spell

It's best to perform this one while the moon is waxing.

For this spell you'll need a candle to represent yourself
in whatever color you think appropriate - a grey candle,
a black candle and an orange candle.

Light the candle that represents yourself and say:
'This is me, me in all things'.
Light the black candle and say:
*'This is all the bad luck that has dragged my footsteps.
Trouble, disappointments and tears are here.
This bad luck now leaves me forever'.*

Light the grey candle and say:
*'All that was bad is neutralized.
All my bad luck is dissolved'.*

Light the orange candle and say:
*'This is the energy coming my way, to get my life moving
and speed up the change'.*

Sit quietly for a while and visualize the negative
energies being whisked into the grey candle and
dissolved into empty nothingness.

Visualize the orange candle drawing good energy and
good luck towards you, see the air stirring about with
possibilities and opportunities.

Let the candles burn down completely (take the usual
safety precautions).

#29 Love Doll To Win Your Love

The best-known way of getting a man to fall in love with you is to bewitch him through a doll that represents him.

Ideally, you should make the doll yourself.

Carve it from some natural material such as wax, wood or clay; bake a doughboy (be sure to use lots of spices), or sew a rag doll.

A store bought figure can be used, but it won't be nearly as powerful as the homemade.

Some very personal belongings of the man you want to enchant, a lock of his hair, a fingernail clipping, something he's worn should be incorporated into, or attached to, the doll.

Add also one of your nail clippings, a strand of your hair, etc.

Use as many of these personal things as possible the more links you create between you, your beloved and the doll, the stronger your spell.

Start the ritual on the first day of the new moon.

Name the doll, aloud, after the man and scratch or write his name on the figure.

Next, using a thorn or pin, gently prick the figure's heart
(don't overdo it) saying:

*"As this thorn (pin) pierces your heart,
so let it be pierced with love for me."*

Or wrap the doll in three ribbons of different colors;
black, white and red are often used, but you may choose
any shades.

As you wrap say:
"Threads bind; body entwine; Heart find linked to mine."

If you've baked your doll, eat a piece of it every night,
saying,

*"As you become part of me,
so let me become part of you."*

Do any one of these rituals, but always the same one, for
fifteen minutes each evening until the moon is full; at
the next new moon, start again.

If he doesn't respond soon enough, light a red candle
and lightly singe the doll's feet, saying:

*"For you I yearn.
For me you burn."*

Before long, his feet should carry him straight to you

When you're not working with your doll, wrap it in a
clean cloth of silk, linen or cotton never a synthetic
fabric and put it away where no one but yourself can
find it.

#30 To Start A Passionate Affair With Thou Person's Desire

Select a candle of light sky blue
And cut seven notches firm and true.

Add to this seven strips of parchment paper,
Placed beside thy candle taper.

Upon them scribe, both first and last
The name of the Lover bold and fast.

Fold the strips in two lengthwise
To keep the names from prying eyes.

Strike a flame and set the candle to burn
And let one strip to ashes turn.

Speak out these words seven times in all,
To summon the forces and with love enthrall:

SPIRIT OF THE DARK LOVE GODDESS DEAR,
BRING (name of desire) TO MY ARMS RIGHT HERE.
LET ME KINDLE THE FLAME OF DESIRE
AND MY LOVE ALWAYS WITH PASSION INSPIRE.

Firm thy vision of what is intended
As the candle to the first notch burns and the hour is
ended.

Repeat this spell a notch each night
And one of the strips gleefully light.

With witches will and concentrated vision
Thou canst capture thy lover with precision.

#31 Lost and Found Spell

To find whatever is lost, chant the following:
Guiding Angels,

I ask your charity,
Lend me your focus and your clarity,
Bring me to the (name of what is lost) at this time,
Restoring me that and my peace of mind.
With harm to none,
This spell be done.
Let it be not reversed,
Or placed unto me as any curse.
May all astrological correspondences
Be correct for this working.
As I will it,
So mote it be.

You should find what you are looking for in a few
minutes to a week.

#32 Balabala's Love Spell

This love spell is intended to attract the perfect mate and partner.

In the circle, ground and center.

Meditate on all the preconceived ideas you have about the perfect partner.

Maybe you have a particular candidate in mind for romance.

Release the thought of that person (it would be most unethical to work magick to make a certain person love you; this would violate their free will, and put you in jeopardy by The Law of Return).

Release all notions of what your perfect lover will look like.

These are externals, and if you cling to them then you run the risk of overlooking your ideal mate simply because your conscious mind was focused on superficialities.

Equipment Needed:
Two candles:
One white
One in your favorite color
Two holders
A rose colored altar cloth
A piece of red chalk

This love spell can be performed at any time. I usually find that the evening is the best.

When your mind is clear and open, hold the candle of your favourite colour - this represents you.

Meditate, then speak aloud all the qualities and energies you are willing to bring to an intimate relationship.

Replace that candle on the altar, and pick up the white one. This represents your ideal partner.

Speak aloud the essential qualities you desire in a mate, and ask Aphrodite to bring you together in this lifetime.

Now place the two candles in their holders at opposite ends of the altar.

Draw a heart on the center with the red chalk, large enough for both candle holders.

Each day thereafter, meditate on the perfect loving relationship for a few minutes, and move the two candles an inch close together.

If you started on the new moon, then by full moon the candles should be touching in the center of the heart.

When they meet, draw two more hearts around the first one, raise energy by singing your favorite love song, and charge the candles.

#33 Basil & Cinnamon Love Talisman

Should be done on a Friday during a waxing moon

Needed:
Large, flat plate
Small picture of yourself
Ground cinnamon
Dried basil
Ceramic or glass bowl
Pink household or taper candle
Small piece of pink cotton cloth
Pink yarn or cord

Hold the candle between your hands & envision yourself as a loving, giving person.

Fill yourself with feelings of love & sensuality.

Infuse those feelings into the candle and then place it in its holder.

Light the candle.

Place the plate before the candle.

Put the small picture of yourself in the middle of the plate.

Pour a small circle of ground cinnamon on the plate around the picture & say:

"Love surrounds me."

Pour a larger circle of basil around the ring of
cinnamon, saying once again:

"Love surrounds me."

Now pour a third, larger circle of cinnamon around the
basil and say once again:

"Love surrounds me."

Hold your hands, palms down, over the three herb
circles and your picture for a few moments.

Sense the energies that are rising from the herbs.

Raise energy.

Visualize again what you want the talisman to
accomplish.
Carefully pour the herbs and the picture into the bowl.

Place your hands into the bowl and mix the herbs with
your fingers, infusing them with your personal energy
as you do so and saying these words or something
similar:

"Spice and herb,
Plant and tree:
send someone to love only thee.
Love we shall share, Equally
As is my will & desire, So mote it be!"

Pour the spices and the picture into the center of the
pink cloth.

Gather up ends and tie them shut with the pink yarn.
Place the love talisman beside the candle.
Let sit there for at least 15 minutes or so as you
concentrate on what you want it to accomplish for you
then pinch out the candles flame.

Burn the candle for at least 7 minutes at approximately
the same time each day and carry the talisman with you
to attract appropriate love.
It is best to make another talisman or recharge this one
about every 6 months or so.

#34 Bring Back my Love Spell

You will need:
2 white candles
A photo of your lover or friend
A photo of yourself smiling
A chamomile teabag
A piece of blue material

To bring back an ex-lover or end an argument between friends.

Perform this spell at 8 o'clock in the evening.

At exactly 8 o'clock light the candles and take a few deep relaxing breaths.

Visualize a peaceful scene.

Now hold in your hand the picture of your ex lover or friend and repeat this chant:

*"With the light of the flame
I'll light your desire,
When I speak your name
You'll feel the glow from my fire.
The spell has been cast--
So be it!"*

Say his or her name slowly 3 times and then put your picture face down on top of his or her picture so that the 2 images are together.

Wrap up the pictures, along with the chamomile tea bag
in the blue cloth.

Put the package in a safe place.

To make sure your ex-lover or friend gets the message,
light the candles and repeat his or her name 3 times
each evening at 8 o'clock.

#35 Bring Someone Close Spell

There are any number of ways to do this spell.

You can drip water (preferably Full Moon Water) on photos of you and your beloved.

You can set a candle in a bowl of water and allow it to burn until the water extinguishes it.

You also may want to use Come To Me oil and/or incense for the spell.

However you do it, visualize your beloved arriving from afar to find your love!

"Sacred water flow from me
To draw him ever near
As endless rivers run to sea
His path to me is clear.
A love that's true once here he'll find
And know his journey's end.
And in his heart and soul and mind
He'll know our lives should blend."

#36 Eye Colour Change Spell

In a dark place, or at night, set two parallel rows of candles, width the space of your outstretched arm, for about 20 to 30 feet, about a foot between candles.

They must be white candles, fresh and never used before.

After the approximately 20 feet, make a circle of candles, with circumference the same as the width of your arms outstretched.

The circle must be southern most.

Light all the candles except a few between the "path" between rows.

Hold with you a white candle, lit, same as the others.

You must also be wearing all white clothes.

Light the candles, and after doing so, kneel before the path, to the south, and ask for a blessing from the gods for your spell.

Walk with the lit candle slowly until you get to the circle, stepping over the unlit ones, turn, now facing the north, and light the candles that were unlit.
(ideally 3 there)

Blow out the candle in your hands, and look at the smoke it makes, feeling your old eye color float away with it.

You can sit or stand at this point, in whatever direction feels comfortable.

Close your eyes, and feel with your spirit all the candles of the circle, and the path.

Focus the light in your eyes, and shift it to the color you want your eyes. when you feel the color staying, and a feeling of completeness,

Open your eyes. blow out the 3 candles to your north, and exit the circle.

Use the candle that you walked with to relight the 3 candles, and blow it out once more.

Walk down the path feeling the power around you, until you get out of the path.

Kneel once more to the south, and thank the gods for their attendance, and one by one, in the order you lit them.

Extinguish the candles.

#37 Truth Spell

Materials:
Thyme,
A Red Candle,
and a Herb dish.

Pour the thyme into the herb dish and say:

*"Purification I do conjure,
So that thoughts be spoke,
No be pondered"*

Light the candle and say:

*"Passion so red,
Set to the fire,
Let the truth be said,
As is my desire"*

Drop red wax onto the herbs and say:

*"Mists of thyme,
Fire of red,
Send the truth to my head"*

Now go to your front door and release the herbs to the wind.

You shall let thyme fly and receive the truth.

#38 Removing Hexes / Curses Spell

Materials:
Old Cooking Pot
Black Candle
Water

Get yourself an old cooking pot, and place a black candle
in the center.

Fill the pot with water until it is 2 inches below the wick
of the candle.

Light the candle and say:

*"If truly hexed or cursed I am, let it break with quench of
flame".*

Then stare into the flame and see all the negative
energy being drawn into it.

When the candle burns down to the water level, and the
flame sputters out, say:

"So mote it!".

Dig a hole and empty the water into it.

Now bury the candle.

It is done.

#39 Reverse A Spell

This is to be used to reverse a spell cast upon a person,
and return the spell upon the one who cast it.

WARNING: Because of the Law of Threes, depending on
the strength of the cast spell, this could cause great
harm to the original spell-caster.

This should only be used in dire need.

You will need a cast iron cauldron, a pile of oak wood,
some mistletoe herb, water and 2.5 pounds of salt.

Collect the hair, nail clippings or anything of the person
upon whom the spell was cast.

Consecrate the ground and cover it with a layer of salt
to prevent evil from interfering.

Pile the Oak wood and light it.

Place whatever was collected from the person into
water in the cauldron and boil.

Add mistletoe and perform an incantation.

The spell is reversed.

As with any spell work, it is best to perform the spell
inside a cast circle for protection.

#40 Speed Up Time Spell

Draw a Pentacle on your left hand
using a blessed red pen.
Visualize a sand clock as you draw.
Now put your left hand on your forehead, or third eye,
and say:

SANDS OF TIME SHOW ME THY WAY
TURN THE NIGHTS INTO DAYS
ROSE PETALS SO LIGHT AND GRACE
SPEED UP TIME NOW, IN THIS PLACE

The spell will last for 24 hours or until the pentacle is
erased, naturally or washed, so try not to get sweaty
hands.

#41 Speed Down Time Spell

Do the same you did in the other one
but with a blue pen and in right hand.
Also do the visualization but with the sands falling
slower, say:

CORE GO ROUND
POWER BE BOUND
INTERUPT THE NATURE'S COURSE
TIME SLOW DOWN
CAST THE SPELL SAIDTH THIS WORDS

The same rules apply to this one.

#42 Love Potion

Needed:
7 ounces Sweet Red Wine
7 Basil leaves
7 Red Rose Petals
7 Apple Seeds
7 drops Vanilla extract
7 drops Strawberry juice
1 Ginseng root cut into 7 equal pieces

By the light of 7 red votive candles, put the 7 ingredients into a cauldron.

Stir the potion 7 times with a wooden spoon each time reciting the following incantation:

*"Let the one who drinks this win
Make his/her love forever mine"*

Bring the mixture to a boil then reduce the heat and let it simmer for seven minutes.

Remove cauldron from the heat and allow potion to cool.

Bless it in the name of Aphrodite seven times; cover and refrigerate until you are ready to serve it to the man or woman whom you desire love and affection.

Word of warning: do not allow anyone other than your beloved to look at, touch or partake of this potion.

#43 Come to me Oil

Used to attract a lover.

Mix equal parts on the following:
Rose
Jasmine
Bergamot
Damiana

After you have finished it, use this oil when you're going on a date.

#44 Perfect Mate Incense

To attract the perfect mate for you at this time in your life.

Red sandalwood 3 parts
Patchouli 2 parts
Orris root 1 part
Dragon's blood 1 part
Lemongrass 1 part

#45 Healing Potion

You need:
2 parts Cinnamon,
2 parts Sandalwood,
1 part Rose petals,
1 part Cayenne,
1 part Ginger,
1 part Rue,
Blue or purple cloth,
(Eucalyptus oil, Chamomile, White Willow bark, or
Wood Betony)

Mix and tie the ingredients in a blue or purple cloth.

Anoint with Eucalyptus oil and wear or place near bed
at night.

Some herbs that are medicinally good for pain relief and
magically good for healing that you might add into the
sachet would be Chamomile, White Willow bark and
Wood Betony.

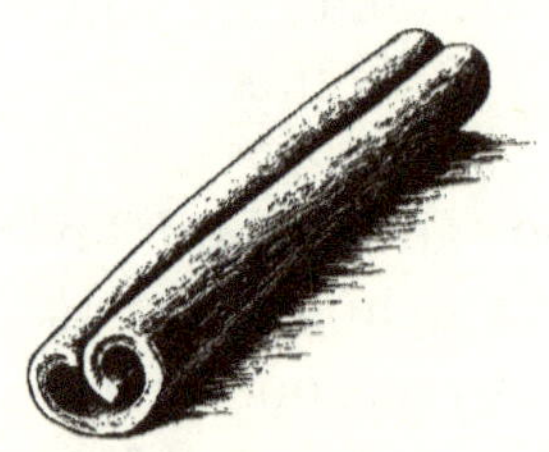

#46 Dream Spell

To dream of a certain person

1 Chunk of Amethyst
3 Rose petals
1 Lock of Hair
1 piece of Daisy Root
1 Drop Rose or Patchouli Oil (optional)
1 Pink Candle (melted so wax binds together)

Take the amethyst, rose petals, lock of hair, daisy root and empower all of them with what you want them to do (in this case, having a magic dream of a lover or friend).

Place the amethyst next to your bed, atop it lay the rose petals, hair (the person of whom you wish to dream of's hair) and the daisy root.

If you wish you may top it all off with rose or patchouli oil and melted pink wax.

To be done during the new moon, right before bed.

While laying down before going to sleep, keep the thought of the person in mind.

#47 Love Spell - Love Charm

Put the following things in a drawstring bag:
1 Rose Quartz,
1 Pink Feather,
and 1/5 Cup of Clove.

Get one pink candle to burn while you're chanting the spell.

Now light the candle and chant the following words:

*"Love shall come to me
by the powers of three,
by my will so shall it be!"*

At this time anoint the bag with holy water and say:

*"The bag is sealed
and the charm is made."*

It is done

#48 The Perfect Soul Mate Spell

Take a shower or bath,
Put on some white clothing.

Take a stick (or your wand) and some glitter outside
where you can see the stars (the best time is a new
moon).

Clear your mind.

Pick up the stick, dip one end into the glitter then raise
the stick towards your chosen star and say:

*"With these magic words
I begin my spell.
Hear me now,
O mystic star,
Hear me well –
Let your magic light
Send me the love of my life.
The spell has been cast –
So be it."*

Your glitter is now magically energized, and you should
sprinkle some near your front door.

You can even take some glitter out with you and
sprinkle it here and there.

Your perfect mate should be brought to you.

#49 Health Spell
Surprising Weight Loss Spell

You need two things:
jasmine essence and a quartz crystal.

Jasmine is the flower of femininity.

I am supposing this magic to be directed to a woman –
of course men do want to lose weight too.

If this is the case, choose and essence such as Patchouli
or Vanilla.

It is the flower of senses, of pleasure, of physical
attraction.

The best suited therefore to bring you back in touch
with the pleasure of being in your skin, looking and
feeling attractive, the feeling that exudes naturally from
a healthy and balanced body.

In fact all the responsibility for weight problems resides
somewhere in the body's loss of its ability to stay
balanced.

Deficiencies on the emotional or mental plane are
interfering with the body's natural wisdom.

When its balance is impaired its happiness is lost.

Through jasmine you may magically evoke that lost
sensuous joyfulness.

With the crystal quartz you focus your energies on the issue at hand and give staying power to the healing forces.

Begin the process during the day when the moon is full.

Cleanse and dress yourself and sit in your magic place.

Place the jasmine flowers or essence and also the quartz crystal in front of you together with the symbols of the elements.

As you call the powers a different element will present itself to you, according to where the imbalance is in you.

That will of course change the shape of the incantation.

In this example I will use the element air – on the basis on this example you can work out the different variations.

So air is in this case the element which speaks, the power which will help you with this magic.
Words belong to air magic.

Now inhale the scent of the jasmine and relax deeply to ask your subconscious to give you a word – the key word for this magic.

For a few minutes you are sitting with your eyes closed, thinking of nothing.

When you sense your mind beginning to wander astray,
touch the quartz – its magical powers will help
immediately to focus your attention again.

Soon the key word will form itself in your conscious
mind: in this example it is "independence".

It does not matter that you understand why this
particular word should be your key word.

Certainly a reason is there, your unconscious has its
own deep wisdom – but it is not important that you
should be consciously aware of its motives.

Every night, from the full moon to the black moon, you
will rub a few drops of jasmine oil on your naked body.

While doing this, let the key word "independence"
stay in your mind.

As you revel in the fragrance of the jasmine, relaxing,
images will come to your mind, suggestions as to how to
expand on the independence in your life.

Maybe you will have a vision on yourself learning a
foreign language.

Following these suggestions is an essential part of this
magic; if you want it to work you will have to find a way.

The quartz will help you with that.

If you find yourself saying "I have too much to do, I
cannot possibly fit this in, I never was good at languages

anyway" etc., touch the crystal and feel its energy for a few seconds.

It will immediately give you clarity and firmness in your purpose, and you will be able to see what you need to do, and have the determination to do it.

Every night, before going to sleep rub the essence on your body and experiment with your key word.

Keep the crystal with you at all times for this period – to touch it whenever you feel that you need to do so.

Thanks to the magic of the flower, of the crystal and of the key word given to you by the power air, a deep change will start in this period.

A change which will enable you to regain your natural balance, and the grace and beauty that go with it.

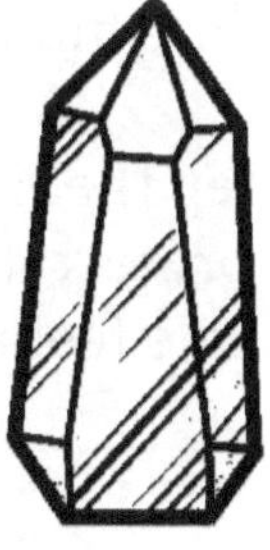

#50 Home Blessng

It is very important for everyone to feel safe and happy within his or her homes.

Feelings of angry or resent not only build up inside of us, but they also build up in our homes.

We have all entered a home that just did not feel safe or warm.

While in that home, the built up energies invaded us, leaving us feeling angry, frightened, or just uncomfortable.

This is not something you want to live with on a constant basis.

The following steps can be performed when doing a home blessing.

The first and most important step is the purification. It will do you little good to bless the home if little angry thought gremlins are hiding in the corner.

Get rid of them; sweep them out into the street. Next bless the home to protect it and bring about warm and safe feelings.

Make your home your sanctuary. The last step would be to set up a permanent household altar that all in the family can use.

This will provide yet another space for magick; no matter what religion your family members follow. You can perform the ritual below or make you own home blessing.

The ritual below is a fill in the blank outline. You may not necessarily want the same things out of your home as I do, so I have left it blank for you to choose.

Purification Supplies:

Incense (purifying scent) and Censer Chalice of Saltwater
Cleaning Supplies
Broom if available

Begin by spending as much time needed to thoroughly clean your home. Get behind that fridge, sweep away those cobwebs on the ceiling, organize your closest. If your walls need a fresh bit of paint go for it.

Why all the cleaning?
Magick must always be reinforced on the physical realm.
What good would it do to get rid of the angry thought gremlins when there are twenty melted lollipops behind the fridge?
Now it is time to work your ritual.

Begin by opening all your windows and doors to allow fresh clean air in.
If you are worried about the neighbors looking in, I don't feel that pulling the blinds would be a problem.

Pick up you broom and visualize yourself sweeping all the negativity out of the house through the open doors. I would begin with the farthest room from the front door so that all the negativity eventually finds its way outside.

Now place your tools upon a table and light the incense. Take a moment feel the energies within the house. Is there any negativity still lingering about? Where is it? What does it feel like? Really tune into the feeling of your home.

Now place your hands over your tools and charge them with the power to cleanse your home. Pick up your chalice and travel clockwise through your house.

Sprinkle the saltwater into every corner of each room, visualize the water washing away negativity, visualize the salt burning the negativity away, and recite:

"By the powers of Earth and Water, I cleanse this house!"

Return to the table and pick up the censer incense.

Take the same route through your home, visualize the smoke clearing away the negativity, and recite:

"By the powers of Fire and Air, I cleanse this house!"

Return to the table. Once again tune into the energies of your house. Is there any negativity still hiding somewhere? If so, repeat the ritual until your home is full of peaceful and calm energies. Now that your home has been purified it is time to bless it. The blessing will help to ensure a safe and happy home.

Supplies needed for blessing:
White candle

Begin in the kitchen of your home, standing in the center of the room.

Tune into the energies of the kitchen, visualize the activities that take place there, or will take place there.

Light the white candle, and visualize the feelings that you would like to find in the kitchen. Send those feelings out through the flame of the candle to spread throughout the room. Recite the following:

*"With this flame,
I fill the room with feelings of____, ____, etc.
This room is protected,
this room is blessed.
So mote it be."*

Continue through the rest of your house in a clockwise direction. Stop in each room, even the bathroom and laundry room, and repeat the process you completed for the kitchen.

Once you have finished with each room, snuff out the white candle and repeat the ritual for the next two days.

Your home is now purified and blessed. The last step is to set up a permanent altar for your entire

family. This altar can be a bookshelf, a cabinet, or a TV stand. Anything will work. I suggest placing in an out of the way area of the home so those working at it will have some privacy.

This will be a family altar; therefore everyone should place something of significance on the altar, even the pets.

Suggestions for altar decorations could be family photos, photos of deceased loved ones, feathers, whiskers from the family cat, a stone found on your honeymoon.

Remember to allow each person to choose their own contribution and respect their choice.

Once the altar has been set up it can be blessed and then decorated for the seasons

www.ingramcontent.com/pod-product-compliance
Lightning Source LLC
Chambersburg PA
CBHW022101150726
47990CB00003B/1195